"Creative, insightful, experiential—this study has been designed with great care. It can take you deeper into the heart of a real pilgrimage with God."

—PAULA RINEHART, author of *Strong Women, Soft Hearts* and *What's He Really Thinking?*

D1378754

A WOMAN'S
JOURNEY OF
DISCIPLESHIP

# Bridges ON THE JOURNEY

## Choosing an Intimate Relationship with Jesus

Gigi Busa
Ruth Fobes
Judy Miller
Vollie Sanders

NavPress is the publishing ministry of The Navigators, an international Christian organization and leader in personal spiritual development. NavPress is committed to helping people grow spiritually and enjoy lives of meaning and hope through personal and group resources that are biblically rooted, culturally relevant, and highly practical.

**For a free catalog go to www.NavPress.com
or call 1.800.366.7788 in the United States or 1.800.839.4769 in Canada.**

© 2010 by The Navigators, Church Discipleship Ministry

All rights reserved. No part of this publication may be reproduced in any form without written permission from NavPress, P.O. Box 35001, Colorado Springs, CO 80935. www.navpress.com. No part of this publication may be reproduced in any form without written permission from The Navigators, Church Discipleship Ministry, P.O. Box 6000, Colorado Springs, CO, 80934. www.navigators.org/cdm.

NAVPRESS and the NAVPRESS logo are registered trademarks of NavPress. Absence of ® in connection with marks of NavPress or other parties does not indicate an absence of registration of those marks.

ISBN: 978-1-60006-786-0

Cover design by Arvid Wallen
Cover images by Shutterstock

The Navigators Church Discipleship Ministry (CDM) is focused on helping churches become more intentional in disciplemaking. CDM staff nationwide are available to help church leadership develop the critical components that will enable them to accomplish Christ's Great Commission. For further information on how CDM can help you, please call (719) 594-2446.

Some of the anecdotal illustrations in this book are true to life and are included with the permission of the persons involved. All other illustrations are composites of real situations, and any resemblance to people living or dead is coincidental.

Unless otherwise identified, all Scripture quotations in this publication are taken from the *Holy Bible, New International Version*® (NIV)®. Copyright © 1973, 1978, 1984 by International Bible Society. Used by permission of Zondervan. All rights reserved. Other versions used include: The Message® (MSG®) by Eugene H. Peterson, copyright © 1993, 1994, 1995, used by permission of NavPress Publishing Group. All rights reserved; the New American Standard Bible® (NASB), Copyright © 1960, 1962, 1963, 1968, 1971, 1972, 1973, 1975, 1977, 1995 by The Lockman Foundation. Used by permission; the *Holy Bible*, New Living Translation (NLT), copyright © 2004. Used by permission of Tyndale House Publishers, Inc., Wheaton, Illinois 60189. All rights reserved; and The Living Bible®, (TLB®) copyright © 1996, used by permission of Tyndale House Publishers. All rights reserved.

Printed in the United States of America

5 6 7 8 9 / 16 15 14

For further information regarding this material and other discipling resources contact:

The Navigators
P.O. Box 6000
Colorado Springs, CO 80934
www.navigators.org/cdm

# CONTENTS

# FROM THE HEART OF THE AUTHORS

A WOMAN'S JOURNEY OF DISCIPLESHIP was written by five women who have experienced firsthand the joy of discipleship and have longed to see God ignite this same passion in others. This three-book series is designed to launch women on their journeys with Jesus, capturing their hearts to follow Him and equipping them to disciple others.

A WOMAN'S JOURNEY OF DISCIPLESHIP is more than a Bible study series; it is a process through which women learn how to walk daily with the Lord and pass on to others that same discipling vision Jesus gave His disciples. Our prayer is that women's hearts everywhere would be ignited to follow Jesus Christ and in turn disciple others, leaving a legacy of spiritual generations. Our hearts are expressed in this verse:

*We loved you so much that we were delighted to share with you not only the gospel of God but our lives as well, because you had become so dear to us. (1 Thessalonians 2:8)*

Will you join us on this great adventure?

# ACKNOWLEDGMENTS

A WOMAN'S JOURNEY OF DISCIPLESHIP is sponsored by the Church Discipleship Ministry, a mission of The Navigators. Leadership training for this series is available. Visit The Navigators at www.navigators.org/cdm for more information. We thank God for those who contributed their ideas, expertise, and prayer throughout the writing process.

# INTRODUCTION

*The revelation of GOD is whole and pulls our lives together. The signposts of GOD are clear and point out the right road. The life-maps of GOD are right, showing the way to joy. The directions of GOD are plain and easy on the eyes.*

(PSALM 19:7-8, MSG)

You are about to embark on the journey of a lifetime. This lifelong adventure will lead you to ~~become more like~~ Christ, loving Him, following Him, and reflecting His love to those around you. As you progress on your journey with Jesus, you will discover Him transforming your mind, emotions, will, and spirit. As you continue to follow God, He will ignite in you a passion for a ministry of discipling others.

A WOMAN'S JOURNEY OF DISCIPLESHIP is laid out as a sequential process covered in three books: *Bridges on the Journey*, *Crossroads on the Journey*, and *Friends on the Journey*. However, each book stands alone and can be used separately.

| | | |
|---|---|---|
| *Bridges on the Journey* | introduces you | to your life in Christ |
| *Crossroads on the Journey* | invites you | to go deeper in your walk with Christ |
| *Friends on the Journey* | equips you | to invest your life in others |

## BRIDGES ON THE JOURNEY

God invites you into a relationship with Him. To begin this relationship, you must cross the bridge of trusting in Jesus and His salvation. After this initial step of faith, you will encounter other bridges that, as you cross them, will help establish your new relationship as God's child. *Bridges on the Journey* will help you form habits and attitudes that will result in intimacy with God, spiritual growth, and fruitfulness as you learn to follow Him daily.

## CROSSROADS ON THE JOURNEY

The second book in the series invites you to take the next step on your journey. New steps often lead to a fork in the path: *Which way should I choose? Crossroads on the Journey* will help you use the Bible as your foremost resource for making daily life decisions. You will have opportunities to develop lifelong convictions to grow even deeper in your relationship with Christ and learn how to pass God's love on to others.

## FRIENDS ON THE JOURNEY

Jesus taught His disciples by example, setting the pattern for His followers. Through your life and ministry, you can learn to encourage and equip others, who will in turn invest their lives in future generations. This final book in the series is intended to empower you with God's vision and passion and give you the skills for a lifelong ministry of discipling others.

## WHAT TO EXPECT IN *BRIDGES ON THE JOURNEY*

All of us are on a spiritual journey. Along the way, many of us will ask deep questions such as "Why do I exist?" and "What is the purpose of my life?" In *Bridges on the Journey*, some of these profound questions will be answered as you come to realize how God is seeking a personal relationship with you and that He has created you to be loved by Him.

*Bridges on the Journey* is designed to help you establish your relationship with Jesus Christ. You will learn how to experience a daily, intimate relationship with Him that will encourage you on your journey. You will also come to understand more of who Jesus is and why He came to earth. As you get to know Jesus better, you will discover more about yourself and about God's relationship with you as His child.

You will also be invited to experience the joy of relating to others in the family of God. Learning, sharing, and growing together are exciting parts of the journey. As you become confident of God's love for you and His purpose for you in His family, you will enjoy security you may never have experienced before.

*Bridges on the Journey* includes the following components:

- **My Daily Journey** is a record of your daily discoveries about God and your-self and a place to share what God has been saying to you each day. My Daily Journey starts at session 3.
- **Our Journey Together** is a time for group members to share recent high-lights from their My Daily Journey pages along with lessons learned on their journeys.
- **Reflections on the Journey** are personal stories from ordinary women about their encounters with an extraordinary God. Their experiences will encourage and motivate you to keep going.
- **The Travel Guide** leads you to a deeper understanding as you explore and experience what the Bible says about your life.
- **Learning the Route by Heart** invites you to memorize God's Word system-atically and allow it to change your life. Bookmarks with each week's memory verses are provided toward the end of the book. Through consistent review of the verses, you will strengthen the vital habit of Scripture memorization.
- **Next Steps on the Journey** gives the assignment to be completed before the next meeting.
- **My Journey Friends** is a record of your fellow group members' names, phone numbers, and e-mail addresses to help you keep in touch with one another. Please take the time during your first meeting to write down this information in appendix A.

Although both the My Daily Journey and Travel Guide sections invite you to spend time in God's Word each week, they have different purposes. The Travel Guide gives you information about your life with God. The My Daily Journey section helps you build your relationship with Him. As you listen to God speak to you from His Word and respond to Him each day in the My Daily Journey section, you will get to know Him better. This practice can continue throughout your life even when you are not doing a formal Bible study.

# GOD'S INVITATION TO THE JOURNEY

## "WHERE AM I ON MY SPIRITUAL JOURNEY?"

*[God] determined the times set for them and the exact places where
they should live. God did this so that men would seek him and
perhaps reach out for him and find him, though he is not far from
each one of us. For in him we live and move and have our being.*

(ACTS 17:26B-28A)

God invites us to journey with Him. Each of our spiritual journeys will be unique. Regardless of where we started the journey, God was already with us, calling us to be His followers and disciples. In this session, you will be invited to know Him in a deeper way than you may have in the past. You will also have the opportunity to learn from one another as you share your stories with each other.

## OUR JOURNEY TOGETHER

In your group:

- Share a little about yourself and your spiritual journey.
- Write the names of your group members on the My Journey Friends pages (see appendix A).
- Taking turns, read the introduction to this book aloud (pages 8–11).

# THE TRAVEL GUIDE

Read Psalm 139:1-4,13-18 (NLT):

*O Lord, you have examined my heart and know everything about me. You know when I sit down or stand up. You know my thoughts even when I'm far away. You see me when I travel and when I rest at home. You know everything I do. You know what I am going to say even before I say it, LORD. . . . You made all the delicate, inner parts of my body and knit me together in my mother's womb. Thank you for making me so wonderfully complex! Your workmanship is marvelous—how well I know it. You watched me as I was being formed in utter seclusion, as I was woven together in the dark of the womb. You saw me before I was born. Every day of my life was recorded in your book. Every moment was laid out before a single day had passed. How precious are your thoughts about me, O God. They cannot be numbered! I can't even count them; they outnumber the grains of sand! And when I wake up, you are still with me!*

1. From the Scripture you just read, what do you observe about God's knowledge of you?

2. These verses in Psalm 139 indicate how God has been with us on our journeys for a long time, even before we recognized Him. Think for a moment about your first memory of God. Tell the group about that memory.

3. Consider where you are now on your spiritual journey. Share about where you'd like to go with God as you continue your journey over the course of this study.

## Next Steps on the Journey

Complete the following assignments before the next meeting:

- Read and complete "Session 2: The Bridge to a Relationship with Jesus."
- Memorize 2 Corinthians 5:17.

# THE BRIDGE TO A RELATIONSHIP WITH JESUS

## "HOW DO I COME TO KNOW JESUS?"

*When someone becomes a Christian, he becomes a brand new*
*person inside. He is not the same anymore. A new life has begun!*
(2 CORINTHIANS 5:17, TLB)

In our last session, we saw that even before we were born, each of us was designed, known, and loved by God. He invites us to respond to an invitation to enjoy a personal relationship with Him.

## OUR JOURNEY TOGETHER

In your group:

- Share personal insights you gained from this session's material.
- Review the memory verse (2 Corinthians 5:17) together.

# Reflections on the Journey

### "Divine Appointments," by Diane Manchester

When I was a child, I attended church with a friend for a few years since my parents didn't go to church. I don't remember much about it, but I know that I liked the free Bible they gave me. I also remember my Sunday school teacher saying, "God is everywhere." That truth was more than I could wrap my mind around. How could God be everywhere?

My transition into high school was a struggle. I remember standing at my open window at bedtime some nights, talking to God through the screen. I guess I thought He couldn't hear me unless my window was open. Yet the truth that "God is everywhere" stuck with me and convinced me that I was not alone as I struggled.

I can look back over the years even before I gave my life to Jesus and see that God had His hand on me. I see His protection when I experimented with high-risk behavior in my early twenties. I also see His provision through particular Christians who spoke to me about Jesus. I remember debating controversial issues with a friend I'd grown up with who had received Christ in her late teens.

About ten years later, my husband and I were living next door to the pastor of a large church. When I was in the hospital, the pastor's wife and her friend visited and gave me a number of Christian booklets. However, at that time I was in such rebellion to "religion" that I dumped them in the closest circular file without even reading them!

I now consider these people "divine appointments" God sent to encourage my spiritual journey. My Sunday school teacher, my childhood friend, and the pastor's wife each had short but high-impact influence for Christ in my life.

Because I grew up in a home without Christ, I had no preconceptions of how to become a Christian. So when God brought trauma into my life that brought me to my knees, my prayer was simple: "I don't know who You are or what You are or if You are, but take this mess that's my life and do something with it!" God was not worried by my naïve words because He knew my heart. He had pursued me for years. He'd sent a string of people who have been ambassadors of His desire to be reconciled to me and bring me to a new life in Christ!

# THE TRAVEL GUIDE

Have you ever seen someone change from the inside out? Many of us can change at least some things on the outside—our behavior, our appearance, our habits—but changing from the inside out can be done only through a relationship with the Lord Jesus. Some of us remember being taught as a child to say, "I'm sorry," when we'd done something wrong. Often, however, "I'm sorry" was only a surface expression that didn't really represent the true feelings in our hearts, so nothing really changed. Soon we were caught in another episode of disobedience when once again we conveyed what was really in our hearts.

When we enter into a relationship with Jesus, we begin to be transformed from the inside out. In this session, we will explore what the Bible says about the promises Jesus makes to us as we take our first steps in this new relationship.

1. Read the following passages. Circle the word *love* every time it occurs, and underline the ways God shows His love to us.

*My beloved friends, let us continue to love each other since love comes from God. Everyone who loves is born of God and experiences a relationship with God. The person who refuses to love doesn't know the first thing about God, because God is love—so you can't know him if you don't love. This is how God showed his love for us: God sent his only Son into the world so we might live through him. This is the kind of love we're talking about—not that we once upon a time loved God, but that he loved us and sent his Son as a sacrifice to clear away our sins and the damage they've done to our relationship with God.* (1 JOHN 4:10, MSG)

*How blessed is God! And what a blessing he is! He's the Father of our Master, Jesus Christ, and takes us to the high places of blessing in him. Long before he laid down earth's foundations, he had us in mind, had settled on us as the focus of his love, to be made whole and holy by his love. Long, long ago he decided to adopt us into his family through Jesus Christ. (What pleasure he took in planning this!) He wanted us to enter into the celebration of his lavish gift-giving by the hand of his beloved Son.*

*Because of the sacrifice of the Messiah, his blood poured out on the altar of the Cross, we're a free people—free of penalties and punishments chalked up by all our misdeeds. And not just barely free, either. Abundantly free! He thought of everything, provided for everything we could possibly need, letting us in on the plans he took such delight in making. He set it all out before us in Christ, a long-range plan in which everything would be brought together and summed up in him, everything in deepest heaven, everything on planet earth.*

*It's in Christ that we find out who we are and what we are living for. Long before we first heard of Christ and got our hopes up, he had his eye on us, had designs on us for glorious living, part of the overall purpose he is working out in everything and everyone. (Ephesians 1:3-12, MSG)*

From the Scriptures you just read, observe and write about God's attitudes, actions, and desire for a relationship with you.

2. What do you see in each passage about God's attitude toward you?

3. What actions has God taken to show you how much He loves you?

God's loving actions toward us demonstrate His desire for us to enjoy a personal relationship with Him. The following Bridge Illustration may help you see how this relationship is made possible.

## The Bridge Illustration

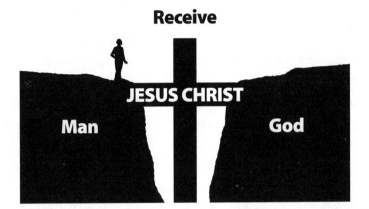

God loves us. He intends for us to experience freedom and purpose in life, yet many of us do not experience an abundant life. Why not? Our problem is that we are separated from God. We chose our own way instead of God's, which created a chasm between Him and us.

On our own there is no way to bridge the gap to God. Good works won't do it. Neither will religion or money or morality or philosophy. Romans 3:23 says, *"All have sinned and fall short of the glory of God."* But God has a remedy. He provided Jesus Christ to bridge this gap. Romans 5:8 says, *"God demonstrates his own love for us in this: While we were still sinners, Christ died for us."*

So how should we respond? We accept God's gift of abundant and eternal life by acknowledging our sins, trusting Christ's forgiveness, and letting Him control our life. John 5:24 says, *"I tell you the truth, whoever hears my word and believes him who sent me has eternal life and will not be condemned; he has crossed over from death to life."* Would you like to cross the bridge and begin your relationship with Jesus now? Here is a simple prayer you can pray to let Jesus know that you want to begin a relationship with Him:

*Dear Lord Jesus, I know that I am a sinner and need Your forgiveness. I believe that You died for my sins. I want to turn from my sins. I now invite You to come into my heart and life. I want to trust and follow You as the Lord and Savior of my life. Amen.*

If you prayed that prayer from your heart just now, you have crossed the bridge and are no longer separated from God. You have begun your relationship with Jesus.

If you didn't pray the prayer, there may be reasons you are not ready to begin a relationship with Jesus today. Perhaps you could talk privately with your group leader or another trusted person about your hesitation. God accepts you right where you are, with your questions, doubts, and anything else that holds you back. Simply ask Jesus to reveal Himself to you as you continue on this journey.

1 John 5:11-13 assures us that we truly have crossed the bridge into life with Christ:

> *This is the testimony: God has given us eternal life, and this life is in his Son. He who has the Son has life; he who does not have the Son of God does not have life.*
> *I write these things to you who believe in the name of the Son of God so that you may know that you have eternal life.*

4. Write out 1 John 5:11-13 in your own words and replace the pronouns with your own name.

Take time now to express your response to God's love and plan for you. Reread the Scripture verses you studied in this session and reply to God in prayer. Don't worry about what words you use or how you sound. God is your friend. Talk to Him as you would talk to a best friend.

# LEARNING THE ROUTE BY HEART

When we travel often to the same destination, there comes a time when we no longer need a map. That's because we've memorized the route by heart. It is similar in our spiritual journeys. When we have God's Word stored in our hearts, it serves as a map to get us through life's challenges and safely to our destination. There are many benefits to memorizing the Scriptures.

Psalm 119:11 says that Scripture keeps us from sin, which is helpful if we want to be like Jesus: *"I have hidden your word in my heart that I might not sin against you."* Psalm 119:105 says that Scripture gives us guidance and direction for our lives: *"Your word is a lamp to my feet and a light for my path."*

Use the tear-out bookmarks provided in appendix D to help you memorize each week's primary verse. Keep the verse with you as you go through your day so you can review it often. Look at it again before you sleep. As you continually keep God's Word in front of you, He will begin to infuse your heart with His wisdom. Plan to review the verse, first saying the topic listed on the bookmark, then the reference, then the verse, and repeat the reference at the end. For example, reviewing your verse for this week would look like this: *"Relationship with Jesus, 2 Corinthians 5:17. 'When someone becomes a Christian, he becomes a brand new person inside. He is not the same anymore. A new life has begun.' 2 Corinthians 5:17."*

There will be one verse provided for each session. At the end of this book, you will have all the verses in your heart, where the Holy Spirit can use them to guide you in every situation on your journey.

**Topic: Relationship with Jesus**
*When someone becomes a Christian, he becomes a brand new person inside. He is not the same anymore. A new life has begun.*
(2 CORINTHIANS 5:17, TLB)

## Next Steps on the Journey

Complete the following assignments before the next meeting:
- Read and complete "Session 3: Believing the Bible."
- Memorize Proverbs 3:5-6 and review 2 Corinthians 5:17.
- Use the My Daily Journey pages in appendix B for your daily devotional time.

# BELIEVING THE BIBLE

## "WHY IS THE BIBLE IMPORTANT IN MY RELATIONSHIP WITH JESUS?"

*Trust in the LORD with all your heart and lean not
on your own understanding; in all your ways acknowledge
him, and he will make your paths straight.*

(PROVERBS 3:5-6)

The Bible is God's personal message to His children. Reading it is the primary way that we come to know and understand who He is and who we are. As we travel on our journeys with Him, His written Word teaches us how to respond to the pressures and demands of daily life.

## MY DAILY JOURNEY

When we travel with others, we get to know them more intimately than before. Jesus chose His disciples and invited them to travel with Him on His journey. During their trip together, they talked, shared their lives, and learned who He was in ways that changed them forever. Jesus set a perfect example for His disciples of what a relationship with our Father can be like. He demonstrated His very personal relationship with God by spending extended time with Him. Mark 1:35 says, *"Very early in the morning, while it was still dark, Jesus got up, left the house and went off to a solitary place, where he prayed."* Jesus and His Father talked together all along Jesus' earthly journey. The My Daily Journey part of each week's session provides the opportunity for you to experience something similar with God.

There is no magic formula for your daily time with God. The purpose is to join your heart with His so He can encourage you. It was Jesus' habit to walk with His Father daily, and that should become the desire of our hearts also. Will you choose to join Him on this journey each day? Begin to meet each day this week with Jesus using your My Daily Journey pages in appendix B as a guide. Please turn there now and read the introduction to the section before beginning at session 3, day 1.

## OUR JOURNEY TOGETHER

In your group:

- Share with one another a highlight you gleaned from My Daily Journey.
- Share personal insights from this session's material.
- Review memory verses together.

## *Reflections on the Journey*

*"Time Well Spent," by Gigi Busa*

*I wish God would give me just one more hour each day! Then I would have time to spend with Him.* Have you ever thought that? Women lead such busy lives. And no matter if we're married or single, just starting out in life or heading toward retirement, there will always be chores, responsibilities, and relationships that demand our time and make us think we don't have time for God. However, I've discovered that time I spend with Him is life-giving and vital. And although Jesus will never insist that I spend time with Him, He longs for it because He loves me.

One of the ways I spend time with God is by reading His Word. Before I began to read the Bible, I thought of God as a harsh and demanding parent. It seemed

He was "up there" keeping a tally and was never quite satisfied. When I began to spend time reading His Word, I saw the true God, and this more accurate perspective transformed my life and relationship with Him and with others.

I discovered the God of the Bible is Abba, the Daddy — God who delights in me and tells me I am so precious that He cannot stop thinking of me. He corrects me gently and lovingly guides me to new areas of growth. When I realized this, I became so excited about His love for me that, just like a toddler, I began running to Him every day, eager to get to know Him better through His Word.

God's fatherly patience and unconditional love became my model for how to love my husband and children. As I experienced God's forgiveness, I was better able to express it to those who had wounded me. My insecurities decreased and my self-confidence grew as I started to see myself from God's perspective. The truths I discovered in His Word became the foundation for my new life in Christ and the plumb line for how I continue to grow.

---

# THE TRAVEL GUIDE

The following is a simple overview of the Bible, the most significant book ever written. It is the account of God's relationship with man. The central figure is Jesus Christ, and the central theme is God's love for each of us expressed through the redemption of man by Jesus Christ's death on the cross.

There is far stronger evidence of the authenticity of the Bible than of any other ancient writing.

God's Word was written by man but inspired by God, as 2 Peter states:

*Above all, you must understand that no prophecy of Scripture came about by the prophet's own interpretation. For prophecy never had its origin in the will of man, but men spoke from God as they were carried along by the Holy Spirit.* (1:20-21)

1. How does this passage establish that Scripture is God's Word?

2. Second Timothy 3:16-17 shows us the sufficiency of God's Word for our lives: *"All Scripture is inspired by God and profitable for teaching, for reproof, for correction, for training in righteousness; so that the man [or woman] of God may be adequate, equipped for every good work"* (NASB).
   a. In what ways does the Bible have the potential to change your life?

## OLD TESTAMENT (39 BOOKS)

| HISTORY | POETRY | PROPHECY |
|---|---|---|
| 17 Books | 5 Books | 17 Books |

| HISTORY — Law | POETRY | PROPHECY — Major Prophets |
|---|---|---|
| 1 Genesis | 1 Job | 1 Isaiah |
| 2 Exodus | 2 Psalms | 2 Jeremiah |
| 3 Leviticus | 3 Proverbs | 3 Lamentations |
| 4 Numbers | 4 Ecclesiastes | 4 Ezekiel |
| 5 Deuteronomy | 5 Song of Solomon | 5 Daniel |

| HISTORY — History and Government | PROPHECY — Minor Prophets |
|---|---|
| 1 Joshua | 1 Hosea |
| 2 Judges | 2 Joel |
| 3 Ruth | 3 Amos |
| 4 1 Samuel | 4 Obadiah |
| 5 2 Samuel | 5 Jonah |
| 6 1 Kings | 6 Micah |
| 7 2 Kings | 7 Nahum |
| 8 1 Chronicles | 8 Habakkuk |
| 9 2 Chronicles | 9 Zephaniah |
| 10 Ezra | 10 Haggai |
| 11 Nehemiah | 11 Zechariah |
| 12 Esther | 12 Malachi |

## NEW TESTAMENT (27 BOOKS)

| HISTORY | TEACHING | PROPHECY |
|---|---|---|
| 5 Books | 21 books | 1 Book |

| HISTORY — Gospels | TEACHING — Paul's Letters | PROPHECY |
|---|---|---|
| 1 Matthew | 1 Romans | Revelation |
| 2 Mark | 2 1 Corinthians | |
| 3 Luke | 3 2 Corinthians | |
| 4 John | 4 Galatians | |
| 5 Acts | 5 Ephesians | |
| | 6 Philippians | |
| | 7 Colossians | |
| | 8 1 Thessalonians | |
| | 9 2 Thessalonians | |
| | 10 1 Timothy | |
| | 11 2 Timothy | |
| | 12 Titus | |
| | 13 Philemon | |

| TEACHING — General Letters |
|---|
| 1 Hebrews |
| 2 James |
| 3 1 Peter |
| 4 2 Peter |
| 5 1 John |
| 6 2 John |
| 7 3 John |
| 8 Jude |

**Notes (between the Testaments):**

There are about four hundred years between Testaments.

The Old Testament looks forward to Christ's sacrifice on the cross.

The New Testament is based on the work of Christ finished on the cross.

b. What are the benefits of living by the Word of God?

In Psalm 19:7-8, God's Word is referred to as *law, statutes, precepts,* and *commands*:

*The law of the LORD is perfect,*
    *reviving the soul.*
*The statutes of the LORD are trustworthy,*
    *making wise the simple.*

*The precepts of the LORD are right,*
    *giving joy to the heart.*
*The commands of the LORD are radiant,*
    *giving light to the eyes.*

3. According to this passage, what adjectives describe God's Word? Which one is most significant to you and why?

When we decide to believe the Bible, we choose to "walk His way" on the journey instead of by our natural impulses. Like Jesus, we learn to trust God's Word rather than our own understanding. When we walk His way, he transforms us, giving purpose and meaning to our lives.

The Bible teaches that God spoke through the Scriptures to reveal Jesus Christ to us. John 1:14 says, *"The Word became flesh and made his dwelling among us."* He is the living Word! He completely, perfectly lived out what the Bible teaches, not only in words but also in actions. Jesus is the living Word of God. He is God's Word spoken to mankind.

4.  Read the following passages about Jesus the living Word and then answer the questions that follow.

*In the beginning the Word already existed.*
    *The Word was with God,*
    *and the Word was God.*
*He existed in the beginning with God.*
*God created everything through him,*
    *and nothing was created except through him.*
*The Word gave life to everything that was created,*
    *and his life brought light to everyone.*
*The light shines in the darkness,*
    *and the darkness can never extinguish it.* (John 1:1-5, NLT)

*He came into the very world he created, but the world didn't recognize him. He came to his own people, and even they rejected him. But to all who believed him and accepted him, he gave the right to become children of God. They are reborn—not with a physical birth resulting from human passion or plan, but a birth that comes from God. So the Word became human and made his home among us. He was full of unfailing love and faithfulness. And we have seen his glory, the glory of the Father's one and only Son.* (John 1:10-14, NLT)

a. What do you think it means that Jesus is the living Word?

b. From these passages, what do you learn about Jesus' identity and origins? How does what you learn influence your understanding about Him?

c. Why do you think "the world didn't recognize him" when Jesus came to earth? Why did His own people reject Him? How receptive are you to truths about Jesus and the Word of God? Has your openness changed over time? How?

d. How do you think these Scriptures will impact your relationship with Jesus?

What do you believe and love about God's Word? Ask Him to help you see how it can give you all you need for life. Pray for His help as you grow in your relationship with Him.

# LEARNING THE ROUTE BY HEART

Our belief in the Word of God as truth must be accompanied by trust in His character. We cannot "lean on our own understanding" (see Proverbs 3:5). In order for us to have straight paths on our journey, we must learn to trust in God's character and goodness and give up thinking that our ways are best. The memory verse for this session helps us keep this important idea always in front of us.

**Topic: Believing the Bible**

*Trust in the LORD with all your heart and lean not on your own understanding; in all your ways acknowledge him, and he will make your paths straight.*

(PROVERBS 3:5-6)

## Next Steps on the Journey

Complete the following assignments before the next meeting:
- Read and complete "Session 4: Experiencing Change in My Life."
- Memorize Matthew 6:33 and review the verses from previous sessions.
- Use the My Daily Journey pages in appendix B for your daily devotional time.

# EXPERIENCING CHANGE IN MY LIFE

## "HOW DOES TRANSFORMATION HAPPEN?"

*Seek first his kingdom and his righteousness,*
*and all these things will be given to you as well.*
(MATTHEW 6:33)

Although Jesus accepts and loves us as we are, the result of His entrance into our lives will be transformation. From the moment when we come into relationship with Him until the day we see Him face-to-face, we will be changing.

The goal of our transformation is to become more like Jesus in every way. The more we are like Him, the more clearly we will reflect Him to others.

## MY DAILY JOURNEY

Use the My Daily Journey pages for session 4 found in appendix B.

## OUR JOURNEY TOGETHER

In your group:

• Share a recent highlight from My Daily Journey.

- Review Proverbs 3:5-6 and your other memory verses.
- Pray together for God to transform your lives.

# Reflections on the Journey

*"Breaking the Chains of Worry," by Gigi Busa*

Have you ever been controlled by fear? I was, for years. My mother had been an anxious woman too, and I assumed that this fearful way of living was normal. I had numerous fears: that people would not like me, that past sins would affect my health and relationships, that I would not create a wonderful home life for my family. My major worry was that someone close to me would die. These fears ruled my life, often affecting my decisions and keeping me from being free. One day I read Matthew 6:25-34, where Jesus addresses worry. Several times He said emphatically, "Do not worry!" I then realized that worrying means that I do not trust God.

Jesus went on to say, "Who of you by worrying can add a single hour to [her] life?" (verse 27). I asked myself, *Does anxiety improve anything in my life?* Worrying had not changed my circumstances, but it sure was wreaking havoc with my sleep and making me uptight and grouchy.

Jesus ended His sermon on worry by saying, "Do not worry about tomorrow, for tomorrow will worry about itself. Each day has enough trouble of its own" (verse 34). My response to Him was, *You're not kidding, Lord!* I realized that focusing on my what-ifs about tomorrow robbed me of the joy I could have today.

I memorized Matthew 6:25-34, and the power of the Word of God and the Holy Spirit began to break the chains of worry that had bound my life. I took each of those fears to Him one by one whenever they came and asked Him for faith to trust Him with my concerns. I pictured placing the person or circumstance in His capable hands. If I started to worry again, I knew I had taken that situation out of His hands. So I would confess my sin and once again place the concern back in His hands.

The result? I am changing: I am becoming a new person, just as God promised.

# THE TRAVEL GUIDE

The transformation process takes place as God teaches us how to live in our circumstances, how to respond to others, and how to experience His presence and involvement in every part of our lives. He directs us through His Word and by His Holy Spirit, who guides us and assures us as we learn to trust and obey God's leadership in our lives.

Just as it takes years for our physical bodies to grow up, it also takes time for us to mature spiritually. But as we obey God's teachings and the Holy Spirit's nudges, we will be surprised to see our natural reactions becoming supernatural — that indeed we are changing!

As we seek God's transformation in earnest, we will discover promises God has given to help and encourage us as we walk purposefully with Him. We will begin to understand who we are, why we are here, and how to live like Jesus.

1. What are the characteristics of the old life and the new life? Read this passage and then fill in the chart that follows it.

   *Live by the Spirit, and you will not gratify the desires of the sinful nature. For the sinful nature desires what is contrary to the Spirit, and the Spirit what is contrary to the sinful nature. They are in conflict with each other, so that you do not do what you want. But if you are led by the Spirit, you are not under law.*

   *The acts of the sinful nature are obvious: sexual immorality, impurity and debauchery; idolatry and witchcraft; hatred, discord, jealousy, fits of rage, selfish ambition, dissensions, factions and envy; drunkenness, orgies, and the like. I warn you, as I did before, that those who live like this will not inherit the kingdom of God.*

   *But the fruit of the Spirit is love, joy, peace, patience, kindness, goodness, faithfulness, gentleness and self-control. (Galatians 5:16-23)*

| CHARACTERISTICS OF THE OLD LIFE | CHARACTERISTICS OF THE NEW LIFE |
|---|---|
|  |  |

2. First Thessalonians 1:5 teaches that mature believers are to be role models for younger believers: *"You paid careful attention to the way we lived among you, and determined to live that way yourselves. In imitating us, you imitated the Master"* (MSG). What do you see in mature believers that you would like to imitate?

3. Romans 12:1-2 explains how transformation takes place in our lives. Read the following passage and then describe the process in your own words.

*Take your everyday, ordinary life — your sleeping, eating, going-to-work, and walking-around life—and place it before God as an offering. Embracing what God does for you is the best thing you can do for him. Don't become so well-adjusted to your culture that you fit into it without even thinking. Instead, fix your attention on God. You'll be changed from the inside out. Readily recognize what he wants from you, and quickly respond to it. Unlike the culture around you, always dragging you down to its level of immaturity, God brings the best out of you, develops well-formed maturity in you.* (MSG)

4. After reading the following three Scripture passages, describe the Holy Spirit's role in transforming your life.

*If you love me, show it by doing what I've told you. I will talk to the Father, and he'll provide you another Friend so that you will always have someone with you. This Friend is the Spirit of Truth. The godless world can't take him in because it doesn't have eyes to see him, doesn't know what to look for. But you know him already because he has been staying with you, and will even be in you!* (John 14:15-17, MSG)

*I'm telling you these things while I'm still living with you. The Friend, the Holy Spirit whom the Father will send at my request, will make everything plain to you. He will remind you of all the things I have told you.* (John 14:25-26, MSG)

*When he comes, he'll expose the error of the godless world's view of sin, righteousness, and judgment: He'll show them that their refusal to believe in me is their basic sin; that righteousness comes from above, where I am with the Father, out of their sight and control; that judgment takes place as the ruler of this godless world is brought to trial and convicted.* (John 16:8-11, MSG)

5. Read 2 Peter 1:3-9 and then complete the chart that follows it. What is God's part and your part in spiritual growth?

*His divine power has given us everything we need for life and godliness through our knowledge of him who called us by his own glory and goodness. Through these he has given us his very great and precious promises, so that through them you may participate in the divine nature and escape the corruption in the world caused by evil desires. For this very reason, make every effort to add to your faith goodness; and to goodness, knowledge; and to knowledge, self-control; and to self-control, perseverance; and to perseverance, godliness; and to godliness, brotherly kindness; and to brotherly kindness, love. For if you possess these qualities in increasing measure, they will keep you from being ineffective and unproductive in your knowledge of our Lord Jesus Christ. But if anyone does not have them, he is nearsighted and blind, and has forgotten that he has been cleansed from his past sins.*

| GOD'S PART | MY PART |
|---|---|
|  |  |
|  |  |
|  |  |
|  |  |
|  |  |

On our journey to believe and follow Jesus, we sometimes become discouraged when we don't seem to be making spiritual progress. Our human nature demands immediate satisfaction. But transformation is a process. Second Corinthians 3:18 puts it this way: *"Our lives gradually [are] becoming brighter and more beautiful as God enters our lives and we become like him"* (MSG).

6. Following are some questions that may come up as you encounter challenges along the way to spiritual maturity. Use the verses provided to answer each question with truth from God's Word.

   a. What should I do when I know I have sinned?

*If we admit our sins—make a clean breast of them—he won't let us down; he'll
be true to himself. He'll forgive our sins and purge us of all wrongdoing.*
(1 JOHN 1:9, MSG)

b. How can I be assured of God's continued love for me?

*With God on our side like this, how can we lose? If God didn't hesitate to put
everything on the line for us, embracing our condition and exposing himself to
the worst by sending his own Son, is there anything else he wouldn't gladly and
freely do for us? And who would dare tangle with God by messing with one
of God's chosen? Who would dare even to point a finger? The One who died
for us—who was raised to life for us!—is in the presence of God at this very
moment sticking up for us. Do you think anyone is going to be able to drive a
wedge between us and Christ's love for us? There is no way! Not trouble, not
hard times, not hatred, not hunger, not homelessness, not bullying threats, not
backstabbing, not even the worst sins listed in Scripture . . .*

*I'm absolutely convinced that nothing . . . absolutely nothing can get between
us and God's love because of the way that Jesus our Master has embraced us.*
(ROMANS 8:31-36,38-39, MSG)

c. What about the times when we feel as though we've failed? How can we know that even then we still belong to God?

*Dear children, let us not love with words or tongue but with actions and in truth. This then is how we know that we belong to the truth, and how we set our hearts at rest in his presence whenever our hearts condemn us. For God is greater than our hearts, and he knows everything.* (1 JOHN 3:18-20)

7. Write a prayer asking God to help you become more like Jesus. Be specific about the ways you need Him to transform you.

In your group time, pray for one another about the areas in which you'd like to grow. Thank the Lord for the changes that will take place as you depend on the Lord Jesus, who has promised to help you moment by moment.

# LEARNING THE ROUTE BY HEART

As you understand and live by the truth of Matthew 6:33 by putting God first in your life, you will experience the results of His promise. For deeper understanding, read Matthew 6:25-34.

**Topic: Transformation**

*Seek first his kingdom and his righteousness, and all these things will be given to you as well.*

(MATTHEW 6:33)

## Next Steps on the Journey

Complete the following assignments before the next meeting:
- Read and complete "Session 5: Living in Relational Community."
- Memorize John 15:12-13 and review the verses from previous sessions.
- Use the My Daily Journey pages in appendix B for your daily devotional time.

# LIVING IN RELATIONAL COMMUNITY

## "WHAT IS MY PLACE IN GOD'S FAMILY?"

*My command is this: Love each other as I have loved you. Greater
love has no one than this, that he lay down his life for his friends.*
(JOHN 15:12-13)

Jesus' sacrifice on the cross for our sin opened the way for us to enjoy God as His child. As we model Jesus' sacrificial love to other believers, our sisters and brothers in the family of God, we will understand the true community God intended, and we will experience profound and lifelong relationships.

## MY DAILY JOURNEY

Use the My Daily Journey pages for session 5 found in appendix B.

## OUR JOURNEY TOGETHER

In your group:

- Share one recent highlight from My Daily Journey.
- Review memory verses from this week and previous weeks.
- Share a concern you would like your friends to pray for.

# Reflections on the Journey

**"Christian Friends: Jesus in the Flesh," by Gigi Busa**

As a new believer in Jesus, I will never forget the way that others loved me and cared for me as I began my new journey of faith. Shortly after starting my journey, I became pregnant with my third child. Morning sickness and fatigue kept me from church and small-group meetings. A dear friend called each week to tell me she had missed me and to keep me informed about our group. After the baby came, I was weighed down with responsibilities. To make it even harder, I often did not have a car on Sundays. This same friend got up earlier on Sunday mornings, got her children ready, and then came to my house to help dress my children and drive us to church.

Although I attended church without my husband, my new friends at church invited my whole family to dinners. Knowing that my husband liked sports, the men at the church invited him to play on the church's softball team. Their consistent Christian character won my husband to the Lord.

I had always had friends, but the friendships I was experiencing as a new believer were deeper and more sacrificial. As I continued to read God's Word and watch my new friends live out Jesus' ways of loving, I was convicted to change my attitudes and actions. I began to pray to see people as God sees them. He reminded me about people I had not forgiven, and as I began to pray for them, I was amazed that the Lord could change our relationships so quickly. I prayed to become a gentle and patient mom to my own three children and several others for whom I provided day care. God helped me see this season of life as a time to invest spiritually in the next generation, and I thoroughly enjoyed it. Keeping up my wardrobe had been a top priority for me, even though we had little money. I learned to buy less and felt blessed to give instead to the church and to others who didn't have much.

Believers are the body of Christ and the family of God. As I experienced early in my journey, believers are "Jesus in the flesh" to one another. Our attitudes and acts of love done in Jesus' power display Him not only to each other but also to a watching world.

# THE TRAVEL GUIDE

No other "god" but our true God has ever called his followers his friends. No other god has ever created them to become his sons and daughters, inheritors with him in the community of those who believe and follow his teachings. Even the majority of the nation of Israel had a limited relationship with God, according to what we read in the Old Testament. Their relationship was one of law and obedience, not the familiarity demonstrated by Jesus toward His Father and toward His followers. Jesus opened up the way for all God's children to enjoy a new kind of fellowship: community with God the Father and with each other.

The common bond between believers is the relationship they share with God through the sacrifice of His Son, Jesus Christ. They share the journey of faith as brothers and sisters in Christ. They long to bring others into this family so they, too, can become part of this body that represents Christ to the world.

The children of God are diverse in every way imaginable, yet their common bonds in Christ, the power of the Holy Spirit, and the grace and love of God bridge any gap that separates them. Let's look at this bridge of relational community on our journey of discipleship.

1. Read John 15:12-15:

   *My command is this: Love each other as I have loved you. Greater love has no one than this, that he lay down his life for his friends. You are my friends if you do what I command. I no longer call you servants, because a servant does not know his master's business. Instead, I have called you friends, for everything that I learned from my Father I have made known to you.*

   a. How does Jesus express His love and friendship to you?

b. In what ways do you demonstrate your love and friendship to Jesus?

2. Jesus has many friends. When Jesus called you His friend (see verse 15), you joined a huge group of other believers who are part of His family. In Scripture, this worldwide group of friends is called "His body" (Ephesians 5:30). Each person is necessary to the whole; we all need one another. The Bible gives us examples of Jesus' friends relating with one another. One especially helpful passage is Acts 2:42-47:

*They devoted themselves to the apostles' teaching and to the fellowship, to the breaking of bread and to prayer. Everyone was filled with awe, and many wonders and miraculous signs were done by the apostles. All the believers were together and had everything in common. Selling their possessions and goods, they gave to anyone as he had need. Every day they continued to meet together in the temple courts. They broke bread in their homes and ate together with glad and sincere hearts, praising God and enjoying the favor of all the people. And the Lord added to their number daily those who were being saved.*

In the early church described in the passage you just read, believers lived their lives together as friends in Christ. How did they demonstrate their devotion to Jesus and to one another?

3. The words fellowship and community come from the Greek word koinonia, which means "sharing in common." The sharing of our lives requires sincere

love, kind speech, continuing encouragement, heartfelt forgiveness, and selfless generosity. How is authentic community demonstrated in each of the following verses?

a. *We love because he first loved us. If anyone says, "I love God," yet hates his brother, he is a liar. For anyone who does not love his brother, whom he has seen, cannot love God, whom he has not seen.* (1 John 4:19-20)

b. *We loved you so much that we were delighted to share with you not only the gospel of God but our lives as well, because you had become so dear to us.* (1 Thessalonians 2:8)

c. *Dear children, let us not love with words or tongue but with actions and in truth. This then is how we know that we belong to the truth, and how we set our hearts at rest in his presence whenever our hearts condemn us. For God is greater than our hearts, and he knows everything.* (1 John 3:18-20)

d. *Let us consider how we may spur one another on toward love and good deeds. Let us not give up meeting together, as some are in the habit of doing, but let us encourage one another—and all the more as you see the Day approaching.* (Hebrews 10:24-25)

e. *If you forgive men when they sin against you, your heavenly Father will also forgive you. But if you do not forgive men their sins, your Father will not forgive your sins.* (Matthew 6:14-15)

f. *Command those who are rich in this present world not to be arrogant nor to put their hope in wealth, which is so uncertain, but to put their hope in God, who richly provides us with everything for our enjoyment. Command them to do good, to be rich in good deeds, and to be generous and willing to share. In this way they will lay up treasure for themselves as a firm foundation for the coming age, so that they may take hold of the life that is truly life.* (1 Timothy 6:17-19)

4. Relationships among believers should be marked by love for each other, which is the very thing that attracts those who do not have a relationship with Jesus. However, our relationship with Jesus does not prevent us from experiencing misunderstandings or differences of opinion. The disciples also argued among themselves and disagreed. Jesus helped His disciples through their conflicts with one another, and God's Word helps us with ours. Scripture is rich in guidance and direction to help us handle the challenges of living in relational community. For example, read Luke 9:46-48:

*An argument started among the disciples as to which of them would be the greatest. Jesus, knowing their thoughts, took a little child and had him stand beside him. Then he said to them, "Whoever welcomes this little child in my name*

*welcomes me; and whoever welcomes me welcomes the one who sent me. For he
who is least among you all—he is the greatest."*

How did the answer Jesus gave the disciples relate to the issue they were arguing
about? How could His words apply to you and your relationships?

5. Read Matthew 5:23-24: *"If you are offering your gift at the altar and there remem-
    ber that your brother has something against you, leave your gift there in front of
    the altar. First go and be reconciled to your brother; then come and offer your gift."*
    According to this passage, how should we respond to a broken relationship with
    a fellow believer? Do you have a broken relationship? What steps can you take
    toward reconciliation?

6. Write a prayer of gratitude for the community you now experience with the
    Father, Jesus, and other believers.

# LEARNING THE ROUTE BY HEART

J esus was our primary example of sacrificial love. We will become the relational community He desired as we expend our lives for the sake of Him and others. Keep that in mind as you memorize this week's verse.

**Topic: Relationships**

*My command is this: Love each other as I have loved you. Greater love has no one than this, that he lay down his life for his friends.*

(JOHN 15:12-13)

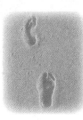

## *Next Steps on the Journey*

Complete the following assignments before the next meeting:

- Read and complete "Session 6: Sharing My Faith."
- Memorize John 3:16-17 and review the verses from previous sessions.
- Use the My Daily Journey pages in appendix B for your daily devotional time.

# SHARING MY FAITH

## "DO I KNOW HOW TO TELL THE STORY OF JESUS?"

*For God so loved the world that he gave his one and only Son, that*
*whoever believes in him shall not perish but have eternal life. For*
*God did not send his Son into the world to condemn the world,*
*but to save the world through him.*

(JOHN 3:16-17)

John 3:16-17 tells the gospel in a nutshell: "God loved us so much that he gave his one and only Son. He sent Jesus to us so that through His death and resurrection we might experience a personal, eternal relationship with Him" (our paraphrase). In this session, we explore how we can share that good news with others.

## MY DAILY JOURNEY

Use the My Daily Journey pages for session 6 found in appendix B.

## OUR JOURNEY TOGETHER

In your group:

- Share one recent highlight from My Daily Journey.
- Review memory verses from this week and previous weeks.

## *Reflections on the Journey*

*"Sharing our Lives and Sharing the Gospel," by Sarah Noyes*

After a long day of school, I pulled into my driveway. New neighbors with two young kids had just moved in next door. I went over and introduced myself and volunteered my babysitting services. From that very first time in their home, Wendi and Matt treated me like family. They included me in their family's special moments. Wendi became a great friend, and Matt treated me as a sister.

My own home was tense even after my parents divorced. Some of their decisions made my life more difficult and left me feeling unloved. To fill this void, I sought any opportunity for momentary happiness. But as I got to know Wendi and Matt, they pointed me to something better.

I loved to visit Wendi and Matt's home. Even during stressful times, their home had a different atmosphere. They always tried to encourage each other. I remember noticing a picture of the cross with the word *freedom* written below it. I thought I'd love to be free from all my emptiness, loneliness, and anger and have peace like Wendi and Matt seemed to have.

Wendi invited me to a Bible study with several of her friends. I didn't understand everything, but as I observed the women honestly sharing their personal challenges, I was amazed they didn't become consumed with their problems. Each of them shared how Jesus had changed her life. I appreciated that these women, like my friends Wendi and Matt, did not make me feel like an outsider.

For my birthday, Wendi and Matt gave me a woman's devotional Bible. A few weeks later, Wendi asked me, "Sarah, what's holding you back from asking Jesus to be your Savior?" I told her I was worried about what my family and friends would think. But even as I answered, I thought to myself, *Why should I let them stop me from knowing Jesus?* At that moment, it was as if God cut through the muddle and grabbed my heart. So then and there, sitting on Wendi's couch, I told Jesus I was a sinner who needed Him.

Later, while reading my devotional Bible, a couple of questions came to mind: *Exactly what do you want from Jesus? Is there some brokenness you would like Him to carry?* As I pondered these questions, the self-protective walls of excuses I had built around my heart came crashing down and I tearfully poured out my heart to Jesus.

Two years later I started a Bible study for high school girls that I still lead today. The girls have lots of questions, and we love our times together, just like Wendi and I do. I'm discipling two of these girls.

By sharing their lives and the gospel with me, Wendy and Matt started me on my journey of discipleship. Even now, I continue to meet with Wendi for discipling. Over time, I left those negative, loveless feelings at the cross. Now I know that Jesus loves me and that He proved it by His death for me. He continues to show His love for me on a daily basis.

———————————

# THE TRAVEL GUIDE

The longer we walk alongside Jesus, the better we get to know His story and the more confident we become in telling His story to our friends. In this section, we will meet two people who encountered Jesus and learn how He changed their lives and the lives of all those around them.

## *The Searching Woman's Story*

She was a woman unacknowledged by men; she was a Samaritan, scorned by the Jews. But as she drew water from a well, a man, a Jew, asked her for a drink. She was surprised, and as they talked, she became even more curious about who He really was. He seemed to know things about her—to understand her past, her present, and even the secret longings of her heart. When He identified Himself as the Messiah, she ran off to tell the townspeople about Him. She said He told her everything she ever did. "Could He be the Christ?" she asked as the townspeople made their way toward Him.

1. Read more about this story in John 4:4-42 and then answer the following questions:

   a. How would you describe this woman?

   b. What do you think she really longed for?

c. When she learned Jesus' identity, where did she go? Why do you think she did this?

d. What impact do you think her story had on the people around her?

### The Blind Man's Story

As Jesus walked along, He saw a man blind from birth. His disciples wondered who was to blame for the man's blindness. Jesus surprised them with His answer and then healed the man. When others, including the Pharisees, saw him healed, they questioned the man and made accusations of Jesus. Even the parents of the healed man did not seem to support him because they were afraid that any association with Jesus would put them out of favor with the religious rulers. The Pharisees did in fact throw the man out of the synagogue, but Jesus went and found him. Jesus told him who He really was, and when the man heard, he believed and worshipped Jesus. Finally the man was made new in both body and spirit.

2. Read more about this story in John 9 and answer the following questions:
   a. Why do you think no one seemed to believe or want to confirm the blind man's story?

b. What did Jesus do when He found the blind man? Why do you think He looked for him?

## *Your Story*

The Samaritan woman and the blind man both had spiritual journeys, but their stories are not much alike, except in one respect: They both encountered Jesus. From that moment on, their lives were changed. Each of us also has a story of our experience with Jesus. Here we will learn how to tell our personal stories in a natural way so that we can share our faith with our friends and family.

3. Write down two or three sentences that describe your life before you trusted Jesus as your Savior. Also answer the following three questions:
   - How was the gospel introduced to you?
   - What was your initial response?
   - When and how did you begin your relationship with Jesus?

4. In two or three sentences, describe the circumstances surrounding your decision to trust Christ. Use the following questions to help you remember:
   - Was I searching for the meaning to life?
   - Was I dealing with a crisis?
   - Was a friend going through life change?

5. Finish your story with two or three sentences about how Jesus continues to change your thoughts and actions since your encounter with Him. Let these questions guide you:
   - Has my hunger for knowing God changed?
   - Am I expressing more Christlike behavior in relationships?
   - Have I experienced changes in my attitude or behavior?

6. Use John 3:16-17 to answer the following questions:
   a. Why do you think God "so loved" the world?

   b. How did God show that love?

   c. Who does God invite to respond to His love?

   d. What does God do for anyone who believes His promise?

   e. How would you explain the phrase "shall not perish but have eternal life" (John 3:16) to a friend?

7. Tell God how you feel about telling your story to your family and friends.

8. List the names of family and friends who need to know God's love. Pray for them by name.

## LEARNING THE ROUTE BY HEART

Only a heart encounter with Jesus will bring real change to our lives. When we genuinely know and walk with Him, we are then able to share this wonderful story with our friends. Reflect on this truth as you memorize this session's Scripture.

**Topic: Sharing My Faith**

*For God so loved the world that he gave his one and only Son, that whoever believes in him shall not perish but have eternal life. For God did not send his Son into the world to condemn the world, but to save the world through him.*

(JOHN 3:16-17)

## *Next Steps on the Journey*

Congratulations! It's time to celebrate your progress on your journey. As a group, plan a time for this celebration. Be thinking about how your weeks together in *Bridges on the Journey* have changed your life so you can share these experiences at your celebration. What are the greatest blessings you received in:

- Your relationship with Jesus?
- Your relationship with others?
- Your friendships in the group?

As new steps often lead to crossroads on your journey, book 2 of this series will inspire you to search deeper within the Bible, the source for making decisions. Through *Crossroads on the Journey*, you will have the opportunity to develop lifelong convictions and grow even deeper in your relationship with Christ. You will also be able to develop new skills for sharing God's love with others.

We invite you to continue your journey in *Crossroads*. You won't want to miss this life-changing opportunity.

# Appendix A

## MY JOURNEY FRIENDS

Record your group members' names, phone numbers, and e-mail addresses in order to keep in touch with one another. As you grow in relationship with the women in your group, you can also record prayer requests.

| NAME | PHONE | E-MAIL | PRAYER NEEDS |
|------|-------|--------|--------------|
|  |  |  |  |
|  |  |  |  |
|  |  |  |  |
|  |  |  |  |
|  |  |  |  |
|  |  |  |  |
|  |  |  |  |
|  |  |  |  |
|  |  |  |  |
|  |  |  |  |
|  |  |  |  |

# My Daily Journey . . .

This section will help you capture your heart's response to reading God's Word. In this first book of A WOMAN'S JOURNEY OF DISCIPLESHIP, you will focus on the life of Jesus as told in the gospel of Mark. As you do so, you will get to know and understand Him better as one who loves you personally.

On any journey, it helps to have a plan. Each My Daily Journey section is broken down into "days" and should be worked on five days of each week, about ten minutes each time. Don't do each session's My Daily Journey pages all at once; work on only one "day" at a time. This will help you build the habit of meeting with Jesus daily.

As you read and reflect on what God says to you, respond by writing your thoughts in a prayer. Use these two questions to guide you:

1. What did I learn about God or myself on my journey?
2. How can I grow deeper in my relationship with the Lord or demonstrate His love to others?

For question 1, record your thoughts. For question 2, respond by writing your thoughts in a prayer. This is what conversation with God is: He speaks to us from His Word and we respond to Him in prayer.

## SESSION 3
### DAY 1 IN MY JOURNEY: MARK 1:1-8

*The beginning of the gospel about Jesus Christ, the Son of God.*

*It is written in Isaiah the prophet:*

*"I will send my messenger ahead of you,*
*   who will prepare your way" —*
*"a voice of one calling in the desert,*
*'Prepare the way for the Lord,*
*   make straight paths for him.'"*

*And so John came, baptizing in the desert region and preaching a baptism of repentance for the forgiveness of sins. The whole Judean countryside and all the people of Jerusalem went out to him. Confessing their sins, they were baptized by him in the Jordan River. John wore clothing made of camel's hair, with a leather belt around his waist, and he ate locusts and wild honey. And this was his message: "After me will come one more powerful than I, the thongs of whose sandals I am not worthy to stoop down and untie. I baptize you with water, but he will baptize you with the Holy Spirit."*

1. What did I learn about God or myself on my journey?

_____

_____

_____

_____

_____

_____

_____

_____

_____

2. How can I grow deeper in my relationship with the Lord or demonstrate His love to others? (Respond to Him in a written prayer, expressing your desires and need for His help.)

_____

_____

_____

_____

## DAY 2 IN MY JOURNEY: **MARK 1:9-11**

*At that time Jesus came from Nazareth in Galilee and was baptized by John in the Jordan. As Jesus was coming up out of the water, he saw heaven being torn open and the Spirit descending on him like a dove. And a voice came from heaven: "You are my Son, whom I love; with you I am well pleased."*

1. What did I learn about God or myself on my journey?

_____

_____

_____

_____

2. How can I grow deeper in my relationship with the Lord or demonstrate His love to others? (Respond to Him in a written prayer, expressing your desires and need for His help.)

_____

_____

_____

_____

## DAY 3 IN MY JOURNEY: **MARK 1:12-15**

*At once the Spirit sent him out into the desert, and he was in the desert forty days, being tempted by Satan. He was with the wild animals, and angels attended him. After John was put in prison, Jesus went into Galilee, proclaiming the good news of God. "The time has come," he said. "The kingdom of God is near. Repent and believe the good news!"*

1.  What did I learn about God or myself on my journey?

_____

_____

_____

_____

2.  How can I grow deeper in my relationship with the Lord or demonstrate His love to others? (Respond to Him in a written prayer, expressing your desires and need for His help.)

_____

_____

_____

_____

## DAY 4 IN MY JOURNEY: **MARK 1:16-20**

*As Jesus walked beside the Sea of Galilee, he saw Simon and his brother Andrew casting a net into the lake, for they were fishermen. "Come, follow me," Jesus said, "and I will make you fishers of men." At once they left their nets and followed him.*
*When he had gone a little farther, he saw James son of Zebedee and his brother John in a boat, preparing their nets. Without delay he called them, and they left their father Zebedee in the boat with the hired men and followed him.*

1. What did I learn about God or myself on my journey?

_____

_____

_____

_____

2. How can I grow deeper in my relationship with the Lord or demonstrate His love to others? (Respond to Him in a written prayer, expressing your desires and need for His help.)

_____

_____

_____

_____

_____

## DAY 5 IN MY JOURNEY: **MARK 1:35-39**

*Very early in the morning, while it was still dark, Jesus got up, left the house and went off to a solitary place, where he prayed. Simon and his companions went to look for him, and when they found him, they exclaimed: "Everyone is looking for you!"*

*Jesus replied, "Let us go somewhere else — to the nearby villages — so I can preach there also. That is why I have come." So he traveled throughout Galilee, preaching in their synagogues and driving out demons.*

1. What did I learn about God or myself on my journey?

_____

_____

_____

_____

2.  How can I grow deeper in my relationship with the Lord or demonstrate His love to others? (Respond to Him in a written prayer, expressing your desires and need for His help.)

_____

_____

_____

_____

## SESSION 4
### DAY 1 IN MY JOURNEY: MARK 2:13-17

*Once again Jesus went out beside the lake. A large crowd came to him, and he began to teach them. As he walked along, he saw Levi son of Alphaeus sitting at the tax collector's booth. "Follow me," Jesus told him, and Levi got up and followed him.*

*While Jesus was having dinner at Levi's house, many tax collectors and "sinners" were eating with him and his disciples, for there were many who followed him. When the teachers of the law who were Pharisees saw him eating with the "sinners" and tax collectors, they asked his disciples: "Why does he eat with tax collectors and 'sinners'?"*

*On hearing this, Jesus said to them, "It is not the healthy who need a doctor, but the sick. I have not come to call the righteous, but sinners."*

1.  What did I learn about God or myself on my journey?

_____

_____

_____

_____

_____

2. How can I grow deeper in my relationship with the Lord or demonstrate His love to others? (Respond to Him in a written prayer, expressing your desires and need for His help.)

_____

_____

_____

_____

_____

_____

_____

## DAY 2 IN MY JOURNEY: **MARK 3:7-12**

*Jesus withdrew with his disciples to the lake, and a large crowd from Galilee followed. When they heard all he was doing, many people came to him from Judea, Jerusalem, Idumea, and the regions across the Jordan and around Tyre and Sidon. Because of the crowd he told his disciples to have a small boat ready for him, to keep the people from crowding him. For he had healed many, so that those with diseases were pushing forward to touch him. Whenever the evil spirits saw him, they fell down before him and cried out, "You are the Son of God." But he gave them strict orders not to tell who he was.*

1. What did I learn about God or myself on my journey?

_____

_____

_____

_____

_____

_____

_____

2. How can I grow deeper in my relationship with the Lord or demonstrate His love to others? (Respond to Him in a written prayer, expressing your desires and need for His help.)

_____

_____

_____

_____

_____

## DAY 3 IN MY JOURNEY: MARK 4:10-20

*When he was alone, the Twelve and the others around him asked him about the parables. He told them, "The secret of the kingdom of God has been given to you. But to those on the outside everything is said in parables so that,*

*"'they may be ever seeing but never perceiving,*
*    and ever hearing but never understanding;*
*otherwise they might turn and be forgiven!'"*

*Then Jesus said to them, "Don't you understand this parable? How then will you understand any parable? The farmer sows the word. Some people are like seed along the path, where the word is sown. As soon as they hear it, Satan comes and takes away the word that was sown in them. Others, like seed sown on rocky places, hear the word and at once receive it with joy. But since they have no root, they last only a short time. When trouble or persecution comes because of the word, they quickly fall away. Still others, like seed sown among thorns, hear the word; but the worries of this life, the deceitfulness of wealth and the desires for other things come in and choke the word, making it unfruitful. Others, like seed sown on good soil, hear the word, accept it, and produce a crop — thirty, sixty or even a hundred times what was sown."*

1. What did I learn about God or myself on my journey?

_____

_____

_____

_____

_____

2. How can I grow deeper in my relationship with the Lord or demonstrate His love to others? (Respond to Him in a written prayer, expressing your desires and need for His help.)

_____

_____

_____

_____

_____

_____

_____

## DAY 4 IN MY JOURNEY: MARK 7:5-8

*So the Pharisees and teachers of the law asked Jesus, "Why don't your disciples live according to the tradition of the elders instead of eating their food with 'unclean' hands?"*

*He replied, "Isaiah was right when he prophesied about you hypocrites; as it is written:*

*"'These people honor me with their lips,*
*but their hearts are far from me.*
*They worship me in vain;*
*their teachings are but rules taught by men.'*

*You have let go of the commands of God and are holding on to the traditions of men."*

1. What did I learn about God or myself on my journey?

_____

_____

_____

_____

2. How can I grow deeper in my relationship with the Lord or demonstrate His love to others? (Respond to Him in a written prayer, expressing your desires and need for His help.)

_____

_____

_____

_____

## DAY 5 IN MY JOURNEY: **MARK 7:14-23**

*Again Jesus called the crowd to him and said, "Listen to me, everyone, and understand this. Nothing outside a man can make him 'unclean' by going into him. Rather, it is what comes out of a man that makes him 'unclean.'"*

*After he had left the crowd and entered the house, his disciples asked him about this parable. "Are you so dull?" he asked. "Don't you see that nothing that enters a man from the outside can make him 'unclean'? For it doesn't go into his heart but into his stomach, and then out of his body." (In saying this, Jesus declared all foods "clean.")*

*He went on: "What comes out of a man is what makes him 'unclean.' For from within, out of men's hearts, come evil thoughts, sexual immorality, theft, murder, adultery, greed, malice, deceit, lewdness, envy, slander, arrogance and folly. All these evils come from inside and make a man 'unclean.'"*

1. What did I learn about God or myself on my journey?

_____

_____

_____

_____

2. How can I grow deeper in my relationship with the Lord or demonstrate His love to others? (Respond to Him in a written prayer, expressing your desires and need for His help.)

_____

_____

_____

_____

## SESSION 5
### DAY 1 IN MY JOURNEY: MARK 12:28-31

*One of the teachers of the law came and heard them debating. Noticing that Jesus had given them a good answer, he asked him, "Of all the commandments, which is the most important?"*

*"The most important one," answered Jesus, "is this: 'Hear, O Israel, the Lord our God, the Lord is one. Love the Lord your God with all your heart and with all your soul and with all your mind and with all your strength.' The second is this: 'Love your neighbor as yourself.' There is no commandment greater than these."*

1. What did I learn about God or myself on my journey?

_____

_____

_____

_____

2.  How can I grow deeper in my relationship with the Lord or demonstrate His love
    to others? (Respond to Him in a written prayer, expressing your desires and need
    for His help.)

    _____

    _____

    _____

    _____

    _____


## DAY 2 IN MY JOURNEY: **MARK 14:3-9**

*While he was in Bethany, reclining at the table in the home of a man known as
Simon the Leper, a woman came with an alabaster jar of very expensive perfume,
made of pure nard. She broke the jar and poured the perfume on his head.*

*Some of those present were saying indignantly to one another, "Why this
waste of perfume? It could have been sold for more than a year's wages and the
money given to the poor." And they rebuked her harshly.*

*"Leave her alone," said Jesus. "Why are you bothering her? She has done a
beautiful thing to me. The poor you will always have with you, and you can help
them any time you want. But you will not always have me. She did what she
could. She poured perfume on my body beforehand to prepare for my burial. I tell
you the truth, wherever the gospel is preached throughout the world, what she
has done will also be told, in memory of her."*

1.  What did I learn about God or myself on my journey?

    _____

    _____

    _____

    _____

    _____

2. How can I grow deeper in my relationship with the Lord or demonstrate His love to others? (Respond to Him in a written prayer, expressing your desires and need for His help.)

_____

_____

_____

_____

## DAY 3 IN MY JOURNEY: MARK 14:17-25

*When evening came, Jesus arrived with the Twelve. While they were reclining at the table eating, he said, "I tell you the truth, one of you will betray me — one who is eating with me."*

*They were saddened, and one by one they said to him, "Surely not I?"*

*"It is one of the Twelve," he replied, "one who dips bread into the bowl with me. The Son of Man will go just as it is written about him. But woe to that man who betrays the Son of Man! It would be better for him if he had not been born."*

*While they were eating, Jesus took bread, gave thanks and broke it, and gave it to his disciples, saying, "Take it; this is my body."*

*Then he took the cup, gave thanks and offered it to them, and they all drank from it.*

*"This is my blood of the covenant, which is poured out for many," he said to them. "I tell you the truth, I will not drink again of the fruit of the vine until that day when I drink it anew in the kingdom of God."*

1. What did I learn about God or myself on my journey?

_____

_____

_____

_____

2. How can I grow deeper in my relationship with the Lord or demonstrate His love to others? (Respond to Him in a written prayer, expressing your desires and need for His help.)

_____

_____

_____

_____

## DAY 4 IN MY JOURNEY: MARK 14:32-42

*They went to a place called Gethsemane, and Jesus said to his disciples, "Sit here while I pray." He took Peter, James and John along with him, and he began to be deeply distressed and troubled. "My soul is overwhelmed with sorrow to the point of death," he said to them. "Stay here and keep watch."*

*Going a little farther, he fell to the ground and prayed that if possible the hour might pass from him. "Abba, Father," he said, "everything is possible for you. Take this cup from me. Yet not what I will, but what you will."*

*Then he returned to his disciples and found them sleeping. "Simon," he said to Peter, "are you asleep? Could you not keep watch for one hour? Watch and pray so that you will not fall into temptation. The spirit is willing, but the body is weak."*

*Once more he went away and prayed the same thing. When he came back, he again found them sleeping, because their eyes were heavy. They did not know what to say to him.*

*Returning the third time, he said to them, "Are you still sleeping and resting? Enough! The hour has come. Look, the Son of Man is betrayed into the hands of sinners. Rise! Let us go! Here comes my betrayer!"*

1. What did I learn about God or myself on my journey?

_____

_____

_____

_____

2. How can I grow deeper in my relationship with the Lord or demonstrate His love
   to others? (Respond to Him in a written prayer, expressing your desires and need
   for His help.)

_____

_____

_____

_____

## DAY 5 IN MY JOURNEY: **MARK 14:55-65**

*The chief priests and the whole Sanhedrin were looking for evidence against
Jesus so that they could put him to death, but they did not find any. Many testi-
fied falsely against him, but their statements did not agree.*

*Then some stood up and gave this false testimony against him: "We heard
him say, 'I will destroy this man-made temple and in three days will build another,
not made by man.'" Yet even then their testimony did not agree.*

*Then the high priest stood up before them and asked Jesus, "Are you not
going to answer? What is this testimony that these men are bringing against
you?" But Jesus remained silent and gave no answer.*

*Again the high priest asked him, "Are you the Christ, the Son of the Blessed
One?"*

*"I am," said Jesus. "And you will see the Son of Man sitting at the right hand of
the Mighty One and coming on the clouds of heaven."*

*The high priest tore his clothes. "Why do we need any more witnesses?" he
asked. "You have heard the blasphemy. What do you think?"*

*They all condemned him as worthy of death. Then some began to spit at him;
they blindfolded him, struck him with their fists, and said, "Prophesy!" And the
guards took him and beat him.*

1.  What did I learn about God or myself on my journey?

    _____

    _____

    _____

    _____

2.  How can I grow deeper in my relationship with the Lord or demonstrate His love
    to others? (Respond to Him in a written prayer, expressing your desires and need
    for His help.)

    _____

    _____

    _____

    _____

## SESSION 6
### DAY 1 IN MY JOURNEY: MARK 15:16-24

*The soldiers led Jesus away into the palace (that is, the Praetorium) and called
together the whole company of soldiers. They put a purple robe on him, then
twisted together a crown of thorns and set it on him. And they began to call out
to him, "Hail, king of the Jews!" Again and again they struck him on the head
with a staff and spit on him. Falling on their knees, they paid homage to him.
And when they had mocked him, they took off the purple robe and put his own
clothes on him. Then they led him out to crucify him.*

*A certain man from Cyrene, Simon, the father of Alexander and Rufus, was
passing by on his way in from the country, and they forced him to carry the cross.
They brought Jesus to the place called Golgotha (which means The Place of the
Skull). Then they offered him wine mixed with myrrh, but he did not take it. And
they crucified him. Dividing up his clothes, they cast lots to see what each would
get.*

1. What did I learn about God or myself on my journey?

_____

_____

_____

_____

_____

_____

2. How can I grow deeper in my relationship with the Lord or demonstrate His love
   to others? (Respond to Him in a written prayer, expressing your desires and need
   for His help.)

_____

_____

_____

_____

_____

_____

## DAY 2 IN MY JOURNEY: MARK 15:25-32

*It was the third hour when they crucified him. The written notice of the charge
against him read: THE KING OF THE JEWS. They crucified two robbers with him, one on
his right and one on his left. Those who passed by hurled insults at him, shaking
their heads and saying, "So! You who are going to destroy the temple and build it
in three days, come down from the cross and save yourself!"*

*In the same way the chief priests and the teachers of the law mocked him
among themselves. "He saved others," they said, "but he can't save himself! Let
this Christ, this King of Israel, come down now from the cross, that we may see
and believe." Those crucified with him also heaped insults on him.*

1.  What did I learn about God or myself on my journey?

_____

_____

_____

_____

_____

_____

_____

2.  How can I grow deeper in my relationship with the Lord or demonstrate His love to others? (Respond to Him in a written prayer, expressing your desires and need for His help.)

_____

_____

_____

_____

## DAY 3 IN MY JOURNEY: MARK 15:42-47

*It was Preparation Day (that is, the day before the Sabbath). So as evening approached, Joseph of Arimathea, a prominent member of the Council, who was himself waiting for the kingdom of God, went boldly to Pilate and asked for Jesus' body. Pilate was surprised to hear that he was already dead. Summoning the centurion, he asked him if Jesus had already died. When he learned from the centurion that it was so, he gave the body to Joseph. So Joseph bought some linen cloth, took down the body, wrapped it in the linen, and placed it in a tomb cut out of rock. Then he rolled a stone against the entrance of the tomb. Mary Magdalene and Mary the mother of Joses saw where he was laid.*

1. What did I learn about God or myself on my journey?

_____

_____

_____

_____

2. How can I grow deeper in my relationship with the Lord or demonstrate His love to others? (Respond to Him in a written prayer, expressing your desires and need for His help.)

_____

_____

_____

_____

## DAY 4 IN MY JOURNEY: MARK 16:1-8

*When the Sabbath was over, Mary Magdalene, Mary the mother of James, and Salome bought spices so that they might go to anoint Jesus' body. Very early on the first day of the week, just after sunrise, they were on their way to the tomb and they asked each other, "Who will roll the stone away from the entrance of the tomb?"*

*But when they looked up, they saw that the stone, which was very large, had been rolled away. As they entered the tomb, they saw a young man dressed in a white robe sitting on the right side, and they were alarmed.*

*"Don't be alarmed," he said. "You are looking for Jesus the Nazarene, who was crucified. He has risen! He is not here. See the place where they laid him. But go, tell his disciples and Peter, 'He is going ahead of you into Galilee. There you will see him, just as he told you.'"*

*Trembling and bewildered, the women went out and fled from the tomb. They said nothing to anyone, because they were afraid.*

1. What did I learn about God or myself on my journey?

_____

_____

_____

_____

2. How can I grow deeper in my relationship with the Lord or demonstrate His love
   to others? (Respond to Him in a written prayer, expressing your desires and need
   for His help.)

_____

_____

_____

_____

_____

## DAY 5 IN MY JOURNEY: MARK 16:9-14

*When Jesus rose early on the first day of the week, he appeared first to Mary
Magdalene, out of whom he had driven seven demons. She went and told those
who had been with him and who were mourning and weeping. When they heard
that Jesus was alive and that she had seen him, they did not believe it.*

*Afterward Jesus appeared in a different form to two of them while they were
walking in the country. These returned and reported it to the rest; but they did not
believe them either.*

*Later Jesus appeared to the Eleven as they were eating; he rebuked them for
their lack of faith and their stubborn refusal to believe those who had seen him
after he had risen.*

1.  What did I learn about God or myself on my journey?

    _____

    _____

    _____

    _____

2.  How can I grow deeper in my relationship with the Lord or demonstrate His love
    to others? (Respond to Him in a written prayer, expressing your desires and need
    for His help.)

    _____

    _____

    _____

    _____

# LEADER'S GUIDELINES

A WOMAN'S JOURNEY OF DISCIPLESHIP is more than a Bible study series. It's a process through which women learn how to walk daily with Jesus and pass on to others that same discipling vision Jesus gave His disciples.

## SUGGESTED FORMAT FOR MEETING

- 10 minutes — Casual interaction.
- 35 minutes — Share from your devotional times, review the memory verse, and talk about experiences or new thoughts that were especially encouraging in walking with Jesus during the previous week. Spend a few minutes praying for one another, particularly about personal insights that came as a result of the present week's session.
- 40 minutes — Discuss the session's material, including reflection stories and Travel Guide.
- 5 minutes–End in prayer.

## GUIDELINES FOR USING *BRIDGES ON THE JOURNEY*

- Allow 60 minutes for session preparation time, not including My Daily Journey. Encourage group members to spend a little time each day to prepare.
- This study can be used one-to-one or in small groups.
- Sessions can be held weekly or biweekly.

# THE LEADER

- The leader should aim to facilitate rather than teach in order to encourage participants to discover truth for themselves.
- We suggest having an assistant leader, who will learn how to lead as she participates with and helps to facilitate a small group.
- The optimum size for small groups is six to eight women. By keeping groups relatively small, each woman is assured of having enough time to be able to share.
- Everyone should be encouraged to do the My Daily Journey pages. This practice is essential for establishing the habit of meeting with the Lord each day.
- At the first meeting, the leader should explain to the group that A WOMAN'S JOURNEY OF DISCIPLESHIP is a process outlined in three books: *Bridges on the Journey, Crossroads on the Journey*, and *Friends on the Journey*. These studies can be done separately, but we recommend going through them in sequence. *Bridges* is designed to help women grow from an initial encounter with Jesus into a deeper understanding of how to walk with Him. *Crossroads* encourages women to make choices that will help them walk consistently with Jesus and grow in spiritual maturity and understanding. *Friends* brings them to a deeper relationship that results in learning how to disciple others.
- None of these books guarantees the making of a believer or a disciple. But the process outlined in the books will provide exposure to life with Christ for those who don't know Him yet and will provide opportunities for believers to become established and equipped in spiritual maturity.
- At the first meeting, the leader should explain what to expect on the journey. Here are the chapter components and how to make the most of them:

  - **My Journey Friends.** At your first gathering, encourage your group to record each other's names, phone numbers, and e-mail addresses in appendix A so you can keep in touch. As relationships grow and deepen, you can also record prayer requests for one another.
  - **My Daily Journey.** Point your group to appendix B, where they can keep

a record of their daily Bible reading times and establish the habit of a daily devotional time.

- **Our Journey Together.** This is a time for group members to share recent devotional highlights **and** lessons learned on their journeys.
- **Reflections on the Journey.** These are personal stories of different women's journeys with Jesus. Each story relates to the particular topic for the week, giving group members the opportunity to learn from another woman's experience.
- **The Travel Guide.** The Travel Guide is a Bible study that group members do on their own during the week. As the women explore the Scriptures and learn new truths, they will experience life change. It's important to emphasize that each woman should complete the study before the group meets so she will be ready to share with others during the group time.
- **Learning the Route by Heart.** This feature provides group members with a systematic plan for memorizing Scripture, allowing God's Word to be stored in their hearts to transform their thinking and behavior. Bookmarks with each week's memory verse are provided in appendix D. By consistent review you will encourage the women to strengthen this vital habit.
- **Next Steps on the Journey.** This is the assignment to be completed before the next meeting.

## CELEBRATION

It's recommended that the leader organize a luncheon or dessert party to celebrate what God has done in the group members' lives. At the end of session 6, set the date and time for this event and invite the women to come with their hearts prepared to share about their journeys with the Lord. Celebrate new and growing relationships with Jesus, new habits of spending daily time in the Bible, and new truths learned about following Jesus in discipleship.

At the conclusion of your luncheon or dessert party, invite group members to continue their study in book 2 of the series, *Crossroads on the Journey.* Share highlights from this second book and tell the women how it could enhance their next steps on their journeys with God.

## ESSENTIALS ON THE JOURNEY

Here are some ideas that we believe are vital to helping women become believers and disciples who follow Jesus all their lives and pass their stories on to others:

- **Small-group relationships.** The focus of your group time should be on developing the women's relationships with Jesus and with each other. Setting an environment of grace and trust allows group members to discover Jesus and be honest in their sharing. Assuring confidentiality is necessary for building trust. This can be instilled in the group by saying simply in each session, "We want each woman to feel comfortable in exploring the Bible and her relationship with Jesus, so please make sure that everything shared in this group stays in this group."

- **Life-to-life.** This means the practice of investing in others from the overflow of your own relationship with Christ. One way you can do to this is by sharing personal examples of God's work in changing your life, developing your character, and empowering you for ministry.

- **Spiritual generations.** When God works through one believer to birth a new generation of believers, we call this a "spiritual generation." God's design is for each generation to pass on to others faith lessons and a profound desire to know and obey Him. Each woman can be a link that reaches into the future. It is inspiring to realize that you are not only impacting the individual women in your group but also influencing the new generations they will reach.

- **Discipleship process.** In each session, emphasize that discipleship is a process. By speaking candidly about your personal continuing growth, you will encourage your group to take the next steps on their own journeys and realize that discipleship is a lifelong endeavor.

# ABOUT THE AUTHORS

GIGI BUSA ministers with the Church Discipleship Ministry (CDM) of The Navigators, partnering with churches to develop disciplemaking leaders. She served on the pastoral staff at Brookville Baptist Church in Holbrook, Massachusetts. Gigi is a speaker who shares her passion for women to develop a dynamic relationship with Jesus. She and her husband, Buzz, live in Massachusetts and adore being parents and grandparents.

RUTH FOBES and her husband, Bob, partner with pastors and church leaders to develop disciples. They have ministered with The Navigators on college campuses and in communities and neighborhoods and presently serve with The Navigators Church Discipleship Ministry. Ruth's great joy has been to see women whom she has discipled and mentored invest in others. The Fobes live in New England and are blessed to be parents and grandparents.

JUDY MILLER serves in ministry along with her husband, Dick. They have been blessed to serve in the Collegiate and Military ministries of The Navigators in the United States and Mexico and within churches where Dick has been the pastor. Judy and Dick now serve with The Navigators Church Discipleship Ministry. Judy's heart is to encourage and disciple women life-to-life in their walk with Christ. She has served as women's ministry coordinator for their church and has been involved in many aspects of women's ministry. They live in Cedar Park, Texas, and are privileged to be parents and grandparents.

VOLLIE SANDERS and her husband, Darrell, have served in The Navigators in Business and Professional, Collegiate, Military, Community, and Church Discipleship ministries. They are presently ministering with the Metro Mission. Vollie was The Navigators' national women's director for five years. Vollie and Darrell live in Colorado Springs, Colorado, and are delighted to be parents and grandparents.

## CHURCH DISCIPLESHIP MINISTRY

CDM is a mission of The Navigators that focuses on helping churches become more intentional in discipleship and outreach. CDM staff help pastors and church leaders develop an effective and personalized approach to accomplishing the Great Commission.

Through a nationwide network of staff, CDM works alongside the local church to build a strong structure for disciplemaking—one that is intentional. Six critical areas are core to an Intentional Disciplemaking Church:

- Mission

- Spiritual Maturity

- Outreach

- Leadership

- Small Groups

- Life to Life

CDM offers seminars, materials, and coaching in these six areas for those interested in becoming an Intentional Disciplemaking Church. See our web page for further information on how CDM can help you.

www.navigators.org/cdm
or email to cdm@navigators.org
or call our CDM Office at (719) 598-1212
or write to PO Box 6000, Colorado Springs, CO 80934

# Continue on your journey of discipleship.

### Bridges on the Journey

Ruth Fobes, Gigi Busa, Judy Miller, Vollie Sanders

*Bridges on the Journey* is a companion to help you and your discipleship group learn the basics of the Christian life — Bible study, living in Christian community, sharing your faith, memorizing Scripture — that will get you started on the right path and keep you going for a lifetime of relationship with Jesus and sharing Him with others.

978-1-60006-786-0

### Crossroads on the Journey

Ruth Fobes, Gigi Busa, Diane Manchester, Judy Miller, Vollie Sanders

*Crossroads on the Journey* takes you deeper in your walk with Jesus, helping you to understand what God has given you through His Word, prayer, and the Holy Spirit to transform your life. Learn what marks a disciple of Jesus, discover your spiritual gifts, and develop the convictions you'll need to persevere in your faith.

978-1-60006-785-3

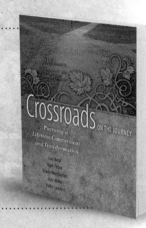

### Friends on the Journey

Ruth Fobes, Gigi Busa, Diane Manchester

Discipleship comes full circle when you pass it on to others in a way that lets them also pass it on. *Friends on the Journey* leads you and your discipleship group into the heart habits, people skills, prayer disciplines, and understandings about God and His passion for the world and love for individuals that will enable you to help women leave behind spiritual generations of people who love Jesus and share Him with others.

978-1-60006-784-6

To order copies, call NavPress at **1-800-366-7788** or log on to **www.NavPress.com**.